A YOUNG POETS MIND

THE RAINBOW NATION IS BLACK

Copyright © 2021 by Visionary Publishers on behalf of a young poets mind (Nonhlanhla Siwela)

All rights reserved.

No part of this publication may be reproduced, stored or transmitted in any form or by any means, electronic, mechanical, photocopying, recording, scanning, or otherwise without written permission from the publisher. It is illegal to copy this book, post it to a website, or distribute it by any other means without permission.

A young poets mind asserts the moral right to be identified as the author of this work.

This body of work contains documented experiences and narratives that some may find offensive or unsettling however it has been written with the intention to provide a sense of healing , inspire critical discourse and inform the reader of social issues particularly those embedded in the African context.

First Publication, 2021
By Visionary Publishers
Houghton
Johannesburg
2198

ISBN: 978-0-620-94930-9

I asked my heart what would make her feel better and she said, "write the book".

"The Rainbow Nation is Black" is how I choose to share my truth. The subcategories "white", "grey" and "black" represent the major social issues, many Africans, including myself, have grappled with and are still trying to grapple with. This is a difficult and ongoing process, but it is necessary because we first need to endure the blackness of the rainbow before we can appreciate the colour.

- A YOUNG POETS MIND

Contents

Foreword	1
White	9
Grey	24
Black	41

Foreword

I do not want this to merely be a book, but an experience. I want us to encounter these narratives together, and navigate the racial tensions, demagogy, and dysphoria we have all felt due to our prescribed identities. We need to unsettle them, interrogate them, resonate with them, then dismantle them. We first need to endure the blackness of the rainbow before we can appreciate the color.

In my journey as a female writer and poet, I have found that there are not many of us. I remember spending a considerable amount of time trying to find books that express womanhood in a woman's voice. I was enthralled when I discovered Chimamanda Ngozi Adichie, Toni Morrison, Alice Walker, Tsitsi Dangarembga, Audre Lorde, Lebo Mashile, Koleka Putuma, Nayyirah Waheed, Rupi Kaur, Sylvia Plath, and Anne Sexton. They became my lifeline. I salvaged the words that I was in the process of massacring within me because they showed me what could happen if I did. There is this unmatched power that words harbor, and it is amplified once a female writer harnesses sit. I have been solely existing but increasingly feeling as though there is a certain emptiness I carry. It was filled once I began writing.

The more I wrote, it was as if I was pouring more into the emptiness, and diminishing its pervading darkness with an inextinguishable light. The process lacked simplicity and writhed uncontrollably with irresistible complexity. I found myself having to grapple with past traumas and reconciling with my perpetrators. May I add that perpetrators do not always have faces and can be in the form of systems.

The notorious patriarchal system became central in most of the pieces I indulged in. I became concerned with rediscovering my identity and redefining my narrative.

The journey began when I read Alice Walker's novel, The Color Purple. I strongly felt that this novel allows for catharsis after catharsis and serves as a catalyst for critical thinking and reimagining. Walker helped me realize that we need to reimagine a lot of things from our country to our schooling, our childhoods, and ourselves. She also taught me about Womanism. This is a term which she first coined. It is the critical cultural, and political strategies and experiences, spiritual and relational practices, attitudes, and modes of expression that distinctively define the lives and liberation struggles of black women in colonial and postcolonial contexts.

One of the first pieces I wrote under this theme are: "Matrilineage" and "Somalia and god". "Matrilineage", explores the issue of motherhood. I did not write this piece to undermine the beauty and grace that is associated with motherhood, but rather I aimed to raise awareness of how many African mothers are subject to familial slavery. I researched how different African languages say "mother", and decided to feature a few to reinforce the objective of the poem. "Somalia and god" should not be read in isolation, but rather as a continuation of "Matrilineage". I explored spirituality in this poem, but also the idea that many little African girls look up to older African women and seek knowledge and teachings from them. This then means that female oppression is cyclical and is culturally entrenched. We need to teach our girls new ways and ideas, and help them to emancipate their own minds from patriarchal influence.

Then came the art of Confessional poetry which is very personal and characterized by the use of "I." This style of writing emerged in the late 1950s and early 1960s. It is associated with poets such as Robert Lowell, Sylvia Plath, and Anne Sexton. Sylvia Plath and Anne Sexton are what I consider legendary female poets amongst many others, of course, but they mastered this type of poetry and have written some of the most intelligent and moving pieces I've ever read. While their treatment of the poetic self may have been groundbreaking and shocking to some readers, these poets maintained a high level of craftsmanship and dismantled the culture of shying away from emotions, feelings, and mental illness. Sexton in particular was interested in the psychological aspect of poetry, having started writing at the suggestion of her therapist. This all sounds morbid, but I think it is crucial to consider as a contemporary female poet or writer.

Although I live in a culture of expression it does not mean that all expression is authentic. I think today's culture is in desperate need of real, raw, and authentic emotional engagement. Emotions and feelings have been romanticized as well as undermined in the media and even in reality. I dared to write as many confessional pieces but I decided that they should not adopt the autobiographical tone or manner previously prevalent in confessional poetry.

That is what birthed "protest poem" , "My own kind", "praise poem", "the police", "If black skin could speak", "My biggest fear" and "the joy parts". In these pieces, I've drawn inspiration from Plath's raw, uncontrived, and even morbid way of expressing and engaging with emotion. Simultaneously, I have drawn inspiration from Sexton's metaphorical style of denouncing a lie and foregrounding her truth. For example, in " My own kind", which I wrote based on Sexton's "Her Kind", I employed a flower as a motif to represent me or any young black woman in a broader sense. I suppose the confession is that I once succumbed to society's limitations imposed on black women. I once carried this inferiority complex with me and listened to a voice in my head that kept saying I would always be less merely because I'm black.

The phrase " I am my Own Kind " is almost paradoxical in that it is apologetic but also assertive. It's like apologizing to myself for listening to the wrong voice, and asserting my true inner voice, my truth, which is capable and powerful. I do not need to conform to be of importance. And I hoped to deliver this message to any black woman who thinks she won't amount to anything. I wanted her to know that she would, and it would be because she embraced and discovered herself and was not so set on wishing she was someone else.

Our society still consists of racists who are extremely terrified of what black people could accomplish if they weren't marginalized. Furthermore, my country in particular still consists of rapists and traditional men who believe masculinity is about asserting power and gaining control over a woman. In writing poems for this collection I realized how important storytelling is and how writing about the documented painful experiences of black Africans is not enough. This then leads to the narrative.

It is the art and practice of telling stories. But not just any stories - life stories. We as black Africans can confess to once being slaves of oppressive systems and limitations. We can confess to conforming to Western standards. But in doing so it erodes our own life stories. We become the oppressed, sometimes the oppressor but never the successor. My poems look at how to take confessional poetry further. How the confession does not need to become one's narrative. But in confessing one can re-write a previously self-oppressive narrative to one that is from the voice of a successor.

This concept was almost lost when Gender-Based Violence surged through our country and ravaged the lives of many women. I remember distinctly the day we held a silent protest at my school for Uyinene. We were paralyzed by pain but I believe her spirit propelled us to go on forward towards justice. Her spirit propelled me to write the piece, "Uyinene is not dead". Although it felt as though my heart would be surmounted by the agony, I wrote. I felt that this was the piece which would chronicle my identity as not just a writer, but as a black female writer. Because many black South African girls, including myself, can see themselves in Uyinene. The possibility of being raped and murdered senselessly is highly likely in my country but justice is not being served. We are not being heard. This and more is why I continue to write as if my very essence shall perish if I do not. It is so to be heard, and not just my own voice or experiences, but those of so many others who share the same narrative and experiences.

It is the difference that I can and have made. The irreplaceable impact in the hearts of many that I have made simply by sharing my truth through my poetry, which compels me each day to carry on. It has brought me here, and I believe it shall take me to many other places in need of the healing and passion my words carry.

And finally, this journey has taught me that a successor is still able to be sentient and soft. The only thing they are not allowed to be is - defeated.

Introduction

The title is a paradox because of course juxtaposing the word rainbow with black is seemingly contradictory. A rainbow is a multicoloured phenomenon, whilst black suggests the absence of colour. And then the nation comes in the middle to add to the confusion, well my thought process behind this was to make critical social commentary. As the rainbow nation do we really celebrate our multicolored nature, our diversity, our differences? Is contemporary South Africa as progressive as we claim it to be? Is it really all colourful or is there still real pain and underlying issues we are yet to address that are threatening to subvert the entire meaning of "Rainbow nation".

Black is not just a colour but black is the space we are afraid to reside in. The space of truth and discomfort. The space where we address the truth about our nation, and how black people in particular are still experiencing exclusion and difficulty with assimilating into contemporary South Africa. The chapters , white , grey and black can be seen as stages or transition phases. White being a stage of oppression and important historical references. It is a call to almost relive those moments of sheer unfairness and division in order to assess whether we have progressed from that stage and also raising to question in what way are we ensuring history does not repeat itself. Grey on the other hand, as we all may be familiar with is 'the grey area', a stage of uncertainty but also possible hope as it recognizes efforts towards progression.

I wanted this to be a chapter of recognizing the importance of moving forward in terms of social justice even when we feel 'stuck'. Black is the final chapter and this represents contemporary South Africa, the transitions we are undergoing, the current political climate, social ills and inequalities we are grappling with and celebratory remarks of the beauty in South Africa or being African in a larger sense. It is the chapter where you realize how necessary the agony is in order to appreciate the harmony that is to come, provided we are willing to come together and reimagine the Rainbow Nation.

White

* * *

Homes

You drove us
   out our homes
   like mealie
   cobs from the soil.

You drove us
   out our homes
   as if we were pests
   from the plantations.

You drove us
   out our homes
   like a wind
   from the mountains.

You drove us
  out our homes
  as if we did not belong,
  as if the land does
  not hold our souls.

You drove us
  out our homes
  and placed an unwelcome
  mat at the door.

aypm

* * *

In this country

We need to stop
  painting all the red flags
  white.

aypm

* * *

It is time

It is

time:

  to purge out white rhetoric,
  to stop whitewashing
  the rainbow nation,
  to stop watching
  when black women
  are dying,
  to be the silver lining by redefining
  our country
  as one that weathers
  racial storms
  by dismantling oppressive norms,
  to stop ignoring
  the scent of historical bloodshed and acknowledge
  each other's wounds instead.

It is time to stop sleeping
  in sheets of sumptuous white satin privilege.

It is time
  to stop sleeping in the sheets
  where women's bodies
  have been
  bleeding.

a y p m

***

They

They keep forcing
oppressive narratives
down our throats
because they fear
that we have
successes to voice.

The successes skewed by the media
and history
like how we built the pyramids of Giza
and were the founders of spirituality
we were the architects
building our way to heaven
they stole our creations
and called our retaliation aggression.

a y p m

***

* * *

To the white boys

To the white boys
   who would never like like me.

   I guess you prefer black girls
   when they come empty spooned
   clean of their blackness like a cantaloupe.

No grittiness.

Not from the hood.

You prefer black girls
   with those affluent accents
   with white neighbors.

   Black girls who go to private schools
   cut off bits of their kink.

Diluted.

Like coconut water.
   The ones who give a damn
   about what you think
   to the extent that they even stumble and falter,
   and then you wonder why we struggle
   to forget the past
   when we must
   constantly be more of you and less of us
   - just to be seen as worthy.

When the best compliment you can give me is
   you're pretty— for a black girl.

   I guess it is partly our fault
   for exalting the thought of having
   a white boyfriend

    for celebrating elaborately when it happens
    posting incessant photos
    building you all these thrones
    willingly giving up our melanin crowns.

We let you bathe in the idea that
    your kingdom is more desirable
    than ours.

And growing up black whilst trying

    to be white
    has shown me how easy
    it is to want
    to swallow and digest
    your own language
    start believing it is barbaric
    trade the irreplaceable magic
    of growing up black
    for the synthetic colonial aesthetic.

Trust me I know,
    and I am still learning and unlearning
    from despising home
    because I began to believe
    that blackness is entrapping
    only to realize that there's nothing more entrapping
    than white systems.

I went from being hypocritical
    to realizing we're all hypocrites in
    all of this
    so to the white boys that would
    never like like me

thank you

    for forcing me to practice
    how to love blackness more.

How to stop
    toning
    it
    down

for you
   how to stop suffocating it
   for you
   how to stop wishing it did
   not exist
   for you
   because if you do not want my
   blackness
you simply do not want me.

I

do not

come

separately.

* * *

Name

You tell me to shorten my name make it simpler for your tongue,
and I hear my ancestors stir in my bones.
I feel an urge deep-seated like sun
to tell you that I am sick to my stomach
of swallowing my magic
turning my existence to a comprehensible brown
washing out the rainbow in me
just for you to always be
the one that shines.

a y p m

* * *

The police

The police
  think our bodies
  are battlegrounds
  they loathe our laughter
  they prefer to hear
  our outcries.

The police
  want to hear
  our eulogies
  they strive to make sure
  that we do not live
  to speak of our victories.

The police
  give too many excuses.

The police
  leave our mothers
  with blood
  on their hands
  and remnants of clothes
  as if enough to mourn
  the loss
  of their child
  an empty house
  with only the ghost
  of their child.

The police
  turn us into corpses.

The police
  deny their senseless killings
  claim to stand for justice
  whilst simultaneously

standing on the bodies
of our lifeless
brothers and sisters.

The police
are threatened by our humanness.

The police
tend to forget
that we have
the resilient spirits
of our ancestors.

a y p m

* * *

Cup of tea

Could you make
me a cup of tea
that would make me
forget about this
compressing quarantine
about the white officers
threatening the safety of the black community,
tea that smells like poetry
replacing the scent of my pungent anxiety,
tea that sounds like rain
as it makes love to my mouth
and caresses my war zone brain.
I despise coffee,
but I need the sleep,
so could you make me a cup of tea,
that is a rich brown,
that feels like love
as it travels down my neck
and my spine.

Tea that fills me with enough peace
  to placate the ambling worry.

Tea that will tell my insides
  everything will be okay
  honey.

a y p m

* * *

The whites fled

the whites fled
  and built their own
  country
  marked their territory
  with each gated community
  high walls
  with louder voices
  than their owners
  the blacks watched
  from a distance
  like animals in a zoo
  suddenly the land we once knew
  became unrecognizable

Mandela's unity
  disintegrated schools became less
  integrated none of us could quite
  understand
  why we preferred to be segregated
  this is how

  -The Rainbow Nation disintegrated

a y p m

* * *

my hair

my hair
  roars
  loud
  it is the lion
  and the mane
  of which both
  you wish to tame
  but my hair
  does not belong
  in your cage
  my hair is mine
  to wear
  without remorse
  and without shame

aypm

* * *

Black Sea

Black Sea,
  you move
  even if the white shore
  tries to inhibit you.
  You prove to the skies
  that you will not fall
  even if they try to drag you down.
  You wear this unapologetic dark,
  mud-like magic
  crown
  on your head;
  you rise instead
  of allowing the pain to

burry you.

Black Black Sea,
  they do not need to see you
  they do not need to feel you
  to know you are coming.
  The birds will sing as if
  showcasing their humming.
  The palm trees will stand tall
  with pride.

You
  like a fearless tide
  will not walk, but stride.
You
  black child
  will become all the tears
  you have cried,
  will overcome all the
  fears you hide,
  will lose it all just
  to find,
  will live even if they think
  you have died.

You
  will.

a y p m

* * *

If you thought
  I was only water
  and that weakness forms my blood.
  I am yet to show you
  that being taken for granted
  only fuels me to become a flood.

a y p m

* * *

We romanticize
how white people
love
and criticize
black people for failing
to give
what they did not receive
enough of at home
we constantly expect
black people to pour
from an empty cup

a y p m

* * *

Butterfly wings

I dream
of my butterfly wings
unearthing
emerging
from being buried

learning how
to straighten
reach for air
breathe
above the surface

I dream
of my butterfly wings
unclipped void
of the white noise
fluttering and flaunting their
exotic naturalistic tones

I dream of my butterfly wings
undid
not bound free

I dream of my butterfly
wings
free

a y p m

* * *

You only fall
when you stop allowing your dreams
to carry you

a y p m

* * *

Grey

***

Only love

Only love
  will bring back the color,
  since all is grey
  and we have tortured
  one another
  for decades,
  since the rainbow nation
  is merely a dream we
  once lived,
  since fear replaces
  the joy in our streets,
  since rape screams relentlessly in our ears.

Only love
  - will bring back peace.

a y p m

***

don't be too busy to love
take advantage of your own
beating heart
share its contents profusely
without fear
without boundaries

a y p m

* * *

when I love
I engulf
your pain becomes
my pain
your joy becomes
my joy
your limbs
join mine
and I walk with you
if your heart splits
in half
I break my own
to make it full again
when you forget to dream
I lose sleep
when you do not believe
I weep
when you grieve
I bleed

a y p m

Leave

leave
  take your rainbow nation
  with you
  take your men
  with you
  take corpses
  with you
  take hate
  with you
  take violence
  with you
  take rape
  with you
  take silence
  with you
  and only return
  when you decide
  to bring love with you

a y p m

***

Love is a task

Love is a task
  in this world,
  because me
  n would rather wage war.
  They would rather kill more,
  and hate more,
  because
  in this world
  love is a task.

a y p m

***

South African Sonnet

There is unrest in Mandela's grave.
There is blood in Mandela's grave.
There is a guest in Mandela's grave.
There is South Africa in Mandela's grave.

There is more than just bones in Mandela's grave
   -because he is still carrying the weight of the country alone.

a y p m

* * *

Dear Mr. President

you have been MIA
and ever since things have not been the same
to say your people are hungry
is an understatement
because South African hunger runs deeper
your people are hungry

and not just for food but for employment ,
ointment for their wounds , a replacement for
their disappointment in you and cabinet
your people are hungry and they need to be fed
but instead they have been mislead
you do not understand that when you first said

God save South Africa they really saw God in you
they really saw a savior in you
but when will you tell them the truth
that saving looks easy and pretty on paper
and you did not sign up for the ugly reality

that requires you to be more than just the mediator
between the private and public sector
because you know your people wonder
if you have stepped outside lately
because you speak as if you have been an
outsider looking in on this country
when you give your practiced speech each night
on the television screen

your people wonder where you have been
like children wondering after their absent father
your people, I mean we
are sorry for being this hungry and clingy its just that
ever since the apartheid saga we have been feeding on
nothing but crust we have been clinging on nothing but dust
and have not had a real conversation since reconciliation
that's why 27 years later they are still serving racism
at the cafeteria in schools

only for it to be consumed again at the dinner table
because South Africa is notorious for not addressing
the elephant in the room
because South Africa is mentally unstable
and we had all this faith in you

like the faith we are told to have in the Bible
like the faith that mother had when she
threw her baby into their hands in the name of survival.

a y p m

* * *

We live in a country

We live in a country
   Where a corrupt leader still has more protection
   than a woman ever will
   where real issues like gender-based violence and poverty
   are not enough to spark controversy

We live in a country
   where most issues are grounds for comedy
   no wonder people are still laughing
   when there are empty bellies that need to be filled
   when there are caskets full of bodies or
   an entire nation that needs to be healed

We live in a country
   where people would rather leave
   than attempt to be a catalyst for change

We live in a country
   where looting as an act of survival is uncivilised
   but looting as an act of greed is justified
   because we live in a country
   where crimes are only Lethal
   when committed by the marginalized

We live in a country
   where voices speak but are only heard
   once they bleed
   we live in a country
   where the freed
   are never really free.

a y p m

* * *

The constitution

The constitution
  promised us an education
  regardless of socio-economic status,
  an education that transcends barriers.

Then why do we need to
  protest
  for what is rightfully ours?
  why are we made to fear
  the very law that claims to protect us?
  why are we gunned down
  when we peacefully ask for what is
  rightfully ours?

The hypocritical nature
  of our legislature
  does not only cost
  us our education but also
  our dignity.

The audacity to
  call us barbaric
  when the university
  demands for us to pay
  our funds in blood,
  but does not account for
  the crime of robbing us
  one by one-
  robbing us of our right
  to be educated in an institution
  that is business orientated
  instead of empathetic.

An institution that claims
  to be inclusive yet religiously
  excludes over 6000 students.
  An institution that abides by
  the constitution when convenient.

An institution that expects us
  to remain silent
  when our brothers and sisters
  are in a crisis.

a y p m

* * *

Youth of 21'

As the youth of 21'
   we still ask ourselves if the fight
   has been won
   if all these years down the line

we find ourselves with no one
   to vote for
   if we study hard just to be turned down
   at every door promising us employment
   if we are told we are the future

but also the country's greatest source
   of disappointment
   if we do not know who we are
   but are constantly confronted
   with the pressure to be someone

a y p m

* * *

I stay even for
the bitter sting
for I know how sweet
your honey can bee

   -The oppressed

a y p m

* * *

Would the Youth of June be proud

When the malicious voice
  of injustice was loud
  they refused to be silenced.

When enslavement
  attempted to hinder their progress
  they persevered as if empowered
  by their ancestors.

When they were told
  to fall at the feet of an unequal government
  they summoned the courage to rise
  in protest.

The youth of June 16 understood the assignment
  they rose up to the challenge
  and conquered.

But,
  would the youth of June 16 be proud
  since we are tone deaf to the sound
  of injustice.

Would the youth of June 16 be proud
  since we live as if the fight is won,
  since we blindly perceive freedom
  as something that now exists for everyone.

Would the youth of June 16 be proud
  since our bones are not shaken
  by the sight of inequality,
  since we have become complacent
  despite the ringing call to challenge
  our government's legitimacy.

Would the youth of June 16 proud,
   since we are not unsettled enough
   to wake up,
   since we are not rattled enough
   to rise,

   since we are not baffled enough
   by the lies
   that all has been done
   and the country is reconciled.

a y p m

                                          * * *

Love II

Love has been missing
   in this world
   I guess she has been clinging
   to the desperate parts
   of our hearts,
   we are so convinced that withholding
   is far better than giving,
   and all that is left is hate
   like thick, impenetrable, grey wind
   engulfing and consuming us.

a y p m

***

We are not dead

We are not dead.
   South Africa still lives within us,
   Uyinene still breathes within us.
   We are silencing the silence.
   We are not deafened
   by the violence.
   Our country is rising
   and we are the limbs.

Black is golden here
it is like glistening coal.
White is cherished here
it is like innocent snow.
We are confronting the grey areas.
We are carrying paintbrushes in our hands
ready to repaint the lands.
We are not dead-
at least not yet.

a y p m

***

Shades of grey to shades of colour

Let us
   share the wars pass around
   the envelope containing difficult questions.

Let us
   encounter raw conversations
   like we encounter fresh cut flowers.

Let us
   smell the wounds like we smell
   the soil when it rains

Let us
   paint portraits with
   the many shades
   of our pain.

a y p m

Africa

I want to be as strong as Africa.
  One day,
  I want to be the hope of many.
  Be their sunrise,
  after seeing a sunset drenched with blood.
  I want to offer my soil of healing
  to any hands that may be needing
  a certain kind of richness to replace
  the greyness -
  the missing minerals in their mines.

I want to be the tea passed around
  during harmless chatter.
  The annoying rooster croaking away
  in the early hours of the morning
  reminding its people that today
  is another chance to live.
  And maybe I do want to be
  as broken as Africa,
  because deep amidst her cracks
  the purest of beauty lives.

She is what keeps an entire nation together.
  She is the pride sitting on the
  High Chief's tongue.
  Oh sweet Africa
  with an old soul.
  Yet a love that is so passionate,
  you would swear she is still young.

a y p m

* * *

Our voices

have become fire -
we can no longer
contain them.

a y p m

* * *

Still, we will rise

Triumph is a narrative
  I wish to whisper
  into our bones even
  when we are grey embers,
  our strength burning away,
  even when we are uncertain
  if we can keep all the mind's fears at bay,
  still,
  even then we are storm,
  powerful even amidst moments
  of stillness the waters,
  will become our tears
  and our witness
  that we can not drown,
  but only become air
  when burdened and hover gracefully
  like clouds above the floods
  with deep-seated defiance,
  effortlessly defying with
  no intended compliance
  the expectations of the crowds
  because like emancipated stars still,
  we will rise.

* * *

Somalia and god

the little Somalian girl
  running through the market
  wants to know
  what god looks like
  bright-eyed
  carrying a war-torn heart
  scraped knees
  panting breathlessly

I search for the words
  whilst she searches through me
  maybe
  god has a ancient voice
  and brown hair
  an exotic feel
  lips bruised with cocoa
  full hips
  the face of a woman
  eyes pouring with compassion
  like the Nile river

I tell her if
  god were here
  she would play the banjo
  smell fresh like
  ripe mango
  make muufo
  and share it with villages
  she would sing you and your
  friends to sleep
  in her eyes, we are all equal

I tell her
  god doesn't forget
  people
  her people forget god

a y p m

* * *

Quarantine and Care

0800 055 555
  (ChildLine and helpline for domestic abuse)
  I am sorry that we couldn't
  be your helpline
  that during this quarantine
  all we could think about
  is our boredom.
  Whilst lives are being torn apart
  because they do not know how
  to salvage an income all we could think about is our
  lack of fun, bodies compressed
  in bars and clubs,
  whilst others are compressed in shacks.
  Maybe that's why lately the rainbow is black.

The colors of humility have seeped
  out and selfishness engulfs our hearts,
  intolerance is falling with abundance
  from the skies and the raindrops are like tears
  full of ash engulfing us all in grey.

The earth has turned into a rotting scab
  and the pus is us.
  We infest and infect everything
  like gangrene and mother nature is angry.
  She is shaking her head in disdain
  as if to say when will we understand
  that we are catalysts
  of chaos but also
  redemption and salvation is in our hands.

That's why the question still stands.
  What are you willing to do
  even amidst the devastation?

a y p m

* * *

Black

***

If black skin could speak
  it would say:

I do not want to die
  with my arms behind my back.

I do not want to die
  with my neck clamped against the tarmac.

I do not want to die
  like a slave.

If black skin could speak
  it would scream it would plead:

I do not want to die please!
  My pores cannot breathe
  because there is hate being
  cemented in their place.

And if white skin could speak,
  It would be silent.
  Because it has never
  seen the need
  - to riot.

a y p m

praise poem

the sun celebrates
when our black skin
glows
Melanin makes flowers
grow
the birds mistake
our hair as
home
the skies exalt
our rich earth
tones
oh to be made with Melanin

a y p m

* * *

protest poem

you might enjoy
  seeing my mouth
  torn open
  in protest to the extent
  of calling it noisy
  to the extent of
  labeling all black women
  as crazy, nasty, and angry

you might find it comical
  to see me rioting
  with my fists up symbolical
  of the strive
  to rid ourselves of the tyrannical
  crimes that still persist today

you want to say
   oh look I told you
   they're always fighting
   pot-belly full of pride
   like a greedy child
   with a mouth-full-of-candy
   at an amusement park
   you find it appropriate
   to mock me
   to shame me just when I think

I can resuscitate my voice
   the one you taught me to
   suffocate and swallow
   the one you only seem
   to recognize on paper
   what you truly wish to say is this

"Oh damn here come those bitter feminists!"

as if stomaching your sick patriarchy
   was meant to be sweet
   as if honey drips from legs
   that have been yanked apart

how dare you speak
   with our blood smeared blatantly
   across your hands
   it almost wants to shriek

"I hate being noticed!"

you might enjoy
   seeing my mouth torn open
   in protest
   but I do not enjoy being oppressed, possessed,
   forcefully undressed, suppressed,
   a product of incest
   because uncles, brothers, cousins,
   and fathers have an insatiable sexual interest
   because they frequently molest
   the ones they're meant to protect

you might enjoy seeing
   my mouth torn open
   in protest
   but this is not a fun parade for me
   this is not a spectacle
   quite frankly
   I'm tired of my genitals
   constantly being put on display
   this is my cortège
   I am here to salvage my dying dignity
   mourn the loss of irreplaceable
   innocence

   you keep bringing me
   your white Jesus
   saying he will show me the way
   and I keep wondering when is the day
   that you'll bring me justice

I guess you might enjoy seeing
   my mouth torn open
   in protest
   so you can say
   black women are the cause
   of the unrest
   but I do not enjoy seeing female
   bodies being slaughtered

I do not enjoy seeing good men
   acting only when it is
   their daughters

a y p m

                              * * *

you kill women
as if they did not breathe life
into you

a y p m

My biggest fear

My biggest fear is to die
  with my legs open
  and my hands up in protest.

My biggest fear is to die
  before my dreams transpire
  because I house a uterus,
  because I bring forth life,
  because men fail to recognize
  the miracle that I am
  as I bleed every month.

My biggest fear is to die
  unnamed
  because there is too many of us,
  to die unheard
  because my voice has been buried
  under the dust of patriarchy,
  a system which says his lust
  matters more than my dignity.

My biggest fear is to die
  with my body gutted
  because a man could not accept
  that he is unwanted.

My biggest fear is to die
  because boys will be boys
  but never real men.

My biggest fear is to die
  because somebody's
  son thinks he is god.

a y p m

* * *

Uyinene is not dead

Uyinene is not
  dead
  I saw her in the crowds
  her silence was so loud
  we could all feel it vibrating
  against our chests
  (rest in eternal love and peace Uyinene,
  she was brutally raped and murdered
  at the post office on the 24th of August 2019)

a y p m

* * *

Matrilineage

Mama
  why is it that when you're
  bleeding we see it as water to drink from
  that when you're needing
  honey and lime
  to soothe your wounds
  why do we assume
  you're made of ointment
  and wine already

Nna
  when last did someone
  kiss your feet
  when last did you
  really eat
  when last were you not afraid
  to speak to let your language
  seep deep into you like

Mzaa
  we've seen you
  as a rope that cannot tire
  for so long
  that even when
  there's something wrong in your heart
  children look past it
  because they're so used to
  you playing your part
  of mother
  equals sufferer.

Mwaitu
  we've heard you
  weeping
  on those days when
  we were meant to be sleeping.

Here.
  Take this poem
  let the words drink
  your magical tears
  dry
  yes you gave us life
  but it does not mean
  you should die
  before your time.

a y p m

                                                * * *

Poem for my mother

My mother wore red pearls
  and thick, leather-like skin.
  Her lipstick looked like
  indelible lines
  piercing within.
  She had wide eyes
  and a broad, invasive chin.

Her bread loaf thighs
  made you despise any edge
  or curve that did not melodically
  dance to what it means to
  be an African woman.
  Yet her strides were defiant
  whilst still retaining a quiet
  gracefully distinctive gait.

As she spoke,
  her words would emanate
  and laminate into your mind.
  She would always elevate
  the standards of benevolence
  for humankind.

She never believed her words were
  articulated with enough eloquence,
  but today I wish she could be a witness
  of the evidence left of what her mindless kindness has done.
  She illustrated the irrelevance
  of modernized accents
  that erode one's mother tongue.

She taught me that socio-economic status
  is a barrier
  that perseverance can overcome

a y p m

* * *

Black women

Black women
  encounter many deaths.
  First, in their childhood homes.
  Then, as they venture
  into a world
  that stifles their joy.

Black women are
  taught that their voice
  is too bold.

Black women are seen as
  offensive even if all they do
  is breathe.

Black women are only
  heard when they
  bleed.

a y p m

* * *

What if

What if
  when we get to heaven
  we see god with the face
  of a black woman,
  her arms decorated
  with a necklace of scars.

What if
  she will be
  wearing a crooked smile
  pulled apart
  by missing teeth.

What if
   god will be beaten
   and tattered, and
   not the white god
   we have all imagined,
   her eyes bulged
   as if carrying stolen sleep,
   her frame hanging weak
   as if belonging to a wrecked house,
   her head bowed
   as if bound to the throne.

What if
   when we get to heaven
   we see god with the face
   of a black woman
   and she howls
   like a mother whose child
   has been riven from her breast
   with rape and murder victims
   postered by her side
   they too howling
   as if in mourning
   drowning under
   black gowns.

What if
   when we get to heaven
   we see that god and her angels
   are actually a prayer band
   of black women
   trying to heal
   from what the world
   did to them.

a y p m

* * *

Woman

She carries survival
  bare on her back
  like an art,
  but you will
  never see it bending
  let alone breaking.

She turns scab marks
  into paintings.
  It is as if
  her strength is
  self-sculptured.

a y p m

* * *

My own kind

I am not a contending flower
  because daffodil does not mean delicate
  and wilting does not mean dead.
  I will not be permeable and porous,
  nor pliable enough
  to eagerly engulf
  the narratives my roots have been fed.

It has been declared.

That my kind
  should remain grounded, unfounded,
  and maintained.
  I have been that kind,

but now

I refuse to be dormant
   prim, poised, and pliant
   merely plucked for my beauty
   because you are so afraid of a woman with talent.
A woman like me
is not afraid to bud.

I am my own kind.

A woman like me
   grows through the mud.
   I am
   my own kind.

a y p m

* * *

the joy parts

they have taught you
   to omit the joy parts
   from your childhood
   to adopt
   the black-homes-are-a-tragedy
   tone
   when you reflect
   on your days at home
   they do not want to hear
   that you enjoyed
   building your own
   toy cars with those
   sandy hands
   and trying on
   your brothers and sisters
   clothes

Instead, they'll pull the words
   we-did-not-have-enough
   from your lips
   and wait for you to
   reduce the love you felt
   as the scent of warm fabric
   hugged your then-still-forming limbs

they will translate that to
   hand-me-downs
   to humiliation
   because they have
   taught you to omit
   the joy parts
   from your childhood
   that all you can recall
   is the leaking-roof
   no-shoes narration

they do not want to hear
   how that same childhood
   strengthened you
   they do not want to hear
   how that same childhood
   welcomed you in ways
   that cannot be found in them

they do not want to hear
   how that same childhood
   birthed dreams
   and not just nightmares

they do not want to hear
   how that same childhood
   fostered resilience
   no,

they do not want to know
how that same childhood
lacked nothing
because
it was so
full

of

joy

a y p m

* * *

Cry, black men, cry

Black men.
  They have swallowed the moon
  and painted their skin
  with black ink from the sun.

Black men.
  They have beautiful fierce
  souls like raging fire and
  arms that glisten like gold
  mines.

Black men are beautiful creatures.
  This is especially true when they cry
  because their tears seem to be pouring
  gloriously
  like the river Nile.

Cry, black men, cry.

a y p m

* * *

Our boys

pretend to be emotionless
because they've been taught by
conflicting cultures
passed on in homes or up
in the mountains
where indoda is synonymous
with stone cold
and this manifests into fits of rage
and ghastly violence
but when will somebody
tell the elders that our boys
are under-age
that our boys are exactly that
boys
that they are like succulents
eager to absorb and store
they cannot sift through the misinformation
because roots do not doubt their source
when will somebody
tell the elders that our boys
need to be taught that
real strength lies in being soft
and in allowing your emotions
to pour

a y p m

* * *

black sister

black sister we are all connected
  the same heart
  beats
  in
  each
  of
  us
the same blood and the same magic
why do you now act
as if this truth is tragic
our hair signifies our resilience
each
braid
a train
of strength
intertwined deep within our roots
the battle has never been
against each other
we do not need to win wars that tear one of us apart
ancestry is not
about simple surnames
ways of speaking
mannerisms
family
it is surplus melanin that binds us like clay
black sister
why did we
ever let
the world's version
of our history
change
the
way
we see each other

a y p m

* * *

black sister II

black sister
  I wonder if these words
  will revive your bones
  compel you to
  drop
  the stones
  of hate
  black sister
  I wonder if these words
  will inspire your soul
  to love your own

aypm

* * *

Zimbabwean lives

  are not sub standard black

aypm

* * *

If you can stand

  for America
  then you can stand
  for Africa

  if black lives truly matter
  then where is the outcry
  for Nigeria.

aypm

All
black

   lives
   still
   matter.
   It was not merely a trend
   for you to passively
   pass on
   to your friends.

a y p m

* * *

Caged birds

Caged birds
   no longer sing
   songs of freedom -
   they sing songs of rage.

   Caged birds no longer
   gaze beyond the bars -
   they break them.

   Blackness is not a death sentence.

a y p m

* * *

I wish

   I wish to be eaten whole
   by the sun, and
   allow the sand to make a home
   in my hair.

I wish to cut my skin melanin bare, then
   collect it in buckets and
   toss it in the streets.

I wish to pack the heaviness
   of being black into boxes and
   leave it in a redemptive titanic
   on its way to island healing.

I wish to breathe in the voices
   of my ancestors and
   wear Khoi San paintings
   as my clothes.

I wish to wear purple to funerals,
   because blackness deserves to live.

I wish to cry myself a river
   of black dreams -
   swim, soak, and bathe in it.

I wish to no longer wish for these things.
   I wish to send prejudice away
   by the flight of handmade
   wings.

a y p m

* * *

Respect black existence
   or expect resistance.

a y p m

* * *

Black woman: She

I had heard
  of a presence like wind
  strikingly subtle
  as if carrying lightning
  in pockets
  always associated with
  male or white

but she
  woman and black as night
  more enchanting than
  dreamy stars
  her hair was wild
  breath pungent as if full
  of proud flowers
  there were elaborate marks
  on her back
  dried black blood engraved between

the cracks
  of her heart
  but it still managed to flow
  with abundant love
  her eyes were home to a
  compassion I had never come to
  know

what a stranger
  the type of encounter
  that tightens your lungs
  yet brings them so much air
  all I could do was stare
  tremble as She wept silently
  because all these many years
  spent denying the possibility

Yes, I
  had not believed
  not even slightly
  that She
  such a marvelous deity
  could ever exist
  fully as me.

a y p m

                        * * *

When you see women
you see god

a y p m

* * *

bring back our girls
who did not get the chance to be women
bring back our women
who did not get the chance
to be girls

a y p m

* * *

Lest we forget
the women in our lives
who like the moon
with their pearlescent radiance
are the light we need
in moments of deep darkness

a y p m

* * *

Pussy

They want my pussy but not my pussy's trauma.
No, they do not want the misogynistic dogma implied,
because it is only enjoyable when the woman complies.
They want my pussy when it is simply a place to come and go
but forget that for me this is a home.
That my pussy is a powerful being,
tearing and mending itself, carrying life so effortlessly.
But how easy it is for them to conveniently omit that part.

They want my pussy with no personality, or history,
my pussy for their pathetic nights.
My pussy with no heart, just tight, and pretty.
They do not want my pussy when she is bleeding or still healing
from intruders who claimed to have good intentions.
They do not want my pussy when she is in needing of a guy with
good intentions. They want my pussy minus the so-called
complications,
minus the humanness, because then it resuscitates their
consciousness.

They want my pussy for the sake of upholding their fragile
masculinity.
They want my pussy but not the responsibility.
They want my pussy, pink and luscious, dripping like passion
fruit infused honey
but not when it is real or scarred from trauma,
not when it demands to be touched gently,
not when it comes with the scent of dignity.

They think my pussy is only worthy of being called art, when it
is porn-star like.
They think my pussy is just a stop for their half-man half-boy
phase,
when they do not want to step up phase,
when they cannot comprehend that my pussy has needs too
phase.

Because you see, they do not want my pussy
unless it is in the merely-there-to-please phase.

They want my pussy as if it is a magazine cutting,
merely for their sighting, an object of interest, a pin on Pinterest.

They want my pussy when it is not afforded respect,
they want it without the baggage of womanhood,
because baggage does not make him feel good.

They want my pussy but not when it is expected that they are educated
about the female anatomy.
They do not want my pussy when it is time to stop calling it pussy.
When it is time to stop reducing its beauty.
When it is time to recognize that it is an honor when a woman gives you,
her body.

They want my pussy wet and sloppy,
not guarded because it is sacred property.
They want my pussy ready for entry, but not when it is ready for safety.
They want my pussy but not my pussy's trauma,
because trauma is heavy and not lacy or sexy.
They want my pussy, but they do not want me,
because somehow the two should come separately.

a y p m

* * *

Dear women (Women's month)

Before I say you are strong. I would like to say you are human.
That is not something the world allows you to be enough.
Before I say thank you for your love. I would like to say you are loved.
Because lately it has not been apparent.
Instead, there is bloodshed from murder rampant and fueled by hate.

The murder of women. The murder of the origin of life.
The murder of lives we all would be nothing without.
You deserve more than just a month of celebration.
You deserve exaltation for the glorious transformations
your sovereign hands have moulded.

The miracle that you are should not go unnoticed.
You have surmounted patriarchal limitations.
And continue to surpass the world's oppressive expectations.

Dear women before I say happy woman's day.
Allow me to say that I am sorry.
I am sorry that your body is constantly mistaken
as belonging to everyone else but you.
I am sorry that your efforts are constantly reduced.
I am sorry that every day you rise heavy laden because nowhere feels safe.

I am sorry for the audacity we've all had to concur that god is male when the power it exudes is the same power that only a woman could.
I am sorry we have all disappointed you in the way we all consciously choose to continuously use instead of continuously appreciate you.

But with this apology please also accept this.

* * *

Dear women.

   You are acknowledged.
   You are appreciated.
   You are exceptional.
   You are beautiful.
   You are meticulous.
   You are sagacious.
   You are significant.
   You are tenacious.
   You are elegant. Lest we forget.

Dear women.
   You are human.

a y p m

* * *

I do not have to
carry your pain
to feel that it is
heavy

a y p m

* * *

For you, African Child

You carry memoirs
of pain
In the crevices of your
spine
but also, a quiet
lightness in the spring
of your step
as if joy has never left
You possess
a strength that is embedded
deep within your bones
but hardly recognized by
the world you behold
you are bold
like a jacaranda tree that
grows espaliered
in the unforgiving
streets of Pretoria
you welcome euphoria
into the air spaces of your lungs
even if life
has chosen to be unkind
even if you have toiled
under the wrath of misfortune
you rise above even when buried
there are many wars
souls such as yours
will encounter and conquer
silently
and that is why you will
always prosper triumphantly

a y p m

* * *

Black community

We fought our way through many hells to be here.
Most of us come from childhoods that left us with scars we cannot heal in this lifetime alone.

Most of us know how far rock bottom can go.
We have archives and scrolls living our bones
documenting stories that sound like legends of how
our ancestors dug their way out of many burials.

Their hands and feet pounding at the earth demanding that she makes way for our community.
We have been hunted, tortured and murdered for our dignity.
Our voices have been silenced.
Our minds have been terrorized and reprogrammed.
Yet we are still the kind of people who only deal with trauma in the grave.

We ridicule the idea of therapy and call it 'the white man's thing'. As if seeking help detracts from the strength us, the melanated, have demonstrated.
We have perfected endurance that we have found ways to hide the scars but that does not diminish their existence.

The black community does not know the difference between self-abuse and self-resilience. That is why most of us suffer in silence because we have been in fight mode all our life.

But when will we stop fighting and sacrificing our mental health?

When will we release ourselves from the many hells we choose to remain in when we refuse to seek help?

a y p m

* * *

you think you've
healed
placed everything into
a neat, labelled box
made sure it's sealed
taken the time to feel
every bit of the trauma
but it somehow finds itself
out and back into you
It sometimes pushes you
so far into the darkest corner
of your mind
that you don't believe
you can find
the light again

   - but you will

a y p m

* * *

About The Author

Nonhlanhla Siwela

I was born in a small town called Pietermaritzburg in Kwa-Zulu Natal. My mother named me Nonhlanhla, which means 'mother of luck'. She gave me this name after her traumatic first pregnancy, she saw me as the light and luck in her life.

I consider myself a bold and multifaceted creative. I completed my high school career at St Johns DSG with an exceptional academic record in 2020 and currently a medical student at the University of Witwatersrand.

I believe strongly in persevering even when faced with adversity, one should not limit themselves, because existence itself is limitless. I am an ever evolving being which can be seen in the way I constantly challenge myself to channel higher vibrational energy, to be the best version of myself.

Nonhlanhla's journey as a writer is compelling and extraordinary, especially considering her tender age. She says, "I did not find poetry, poetry found me" and she never ceases to wholeheartedly embrace her artistry.

www.ingramcontent.com/pod-product-compliance
Lightning Source LLC
Chambersburg PA
CBHW022109160426
43198CB00008B/414